THE LITTLE LIBRARY OF EARTH MEDICINE

OWL

Kenneth Meadows

Illustrations by Jo Donegan

DORLING KINDERSLEY
LONDON • NEW YORK • SYDNEY • MOSCOW

A DORLING KINDERSLEY BOOK

Managing editor: Jonathan Metcalf
Managing art editor: Peter Cross
Production manager: Michelle Thomas

The Little Library of Earth Medicine was
produced, edited and designed by
GLS Editorial and Design
Garden Studios, 11-15 Betterton Street
London WC2H 9BP

GLS Editorial and Design
Editorial director: Jane Laing
Design director: Ruth Shane
Project designer: Luke Herriott
Editors: Claire Calman, Terry Burrows, Victoria Sorzano

Additional illustrations: Roy Flooks 16, 17, 31; John Lawrence 38
Special photography: Mark Hamilton
Picture credits: American Natural History Museum 8-9, 12, 14-15, 32

First published in Great Britain in 1998
by Dorling Kindersley Limited
9 Henrietta Street, London WC2E 8PS

2 4 6 8 10 9 7 5 3 1

A CIP catalogue record for this book is available from the British Library

UK ISBN 0 7513 0522 7   AUSTRALIAN ISBN 1 86466 039 2

Reproduced by Kestrel Digital Colour Ltd, Chelmsford, Essex
Printed and bound in Hong Kong by Imago

CONTENTS

Introducing Earth Medicine 8
The Medicine Wheel 10
The Twelve Birth Times 12
The Significance of Totems 14
The Twelve Birth Totems 16
The Influence of the Directions 18
The Influence of the Elements 20
The Influence of the Moon 22
The Influence of Energy Flow 24

Owl Medicine 25

Season of Birth: Long Nights Time 26
Birth Totem: The Owl 28
The Owl and Relationships 30
Directional Totem: The Grizzly Bear 32
Elemental Totem: The Hawk 34
Stone Affinity: Obsidian 36
Tree Affinity: Honeysuckle 38
Colour Affinity; Gold 40
Working the Wheel: Life Path 42
Working the Wheel: Medicine Power 44

INTRODUCING
EARTH MEDICINE

TO NATIVE AMERICANS, MEDICINE IS NOT AN EXTERNAL
SUBSTANCE BUT AN INNER POWER THAT IS FOUND IN
BOTH NATURE AND OURSELVES.

Earth Medicine is a unique method of personality profiling that draws on Native American understanding of the Universe, and on the principles embodied in sacred Medicine Wheels.

Native Americans believed that spirit, although invisible, permeated Nature, so that everything in Nature was sacred. Animals were perceived as acting as

Shaman's rattle
Shamans used rattles to connect with their inner spirit. This is a Tlingit shaman's wooden rattle.

messengers of spirit. They also appeared in waking dreams to impart power known as "medicine." The recipients of such dreams honoured the animal species that appeared to them by rendering their images on ceremonial, ornamental, and everyday artifacts.

NATURE WITHIN SELF
Native American shamans – tribal wisemen – recognized similarities between the natural forces prevalent during the seasons and the characteristics of those born

"Spirit has provided you with an opportunity to study in Nature's university." Stoney teaching

during corresponding times of the year. They also noted how personality is affected by the four phases of the Moon – at birth and throughout life – and by the continual alternation of energy flow, from active to passive. This view is encapsulated in Earth Medicine, which helps you to recognize how the dynamics of Nature function within you and how the potential strengths you were born with can be developed.

MEDICINE WHEELS

Native American cultural traditions embrace a variety of circular symbolic images and objects. These sacred hoops have become known as Medicine

Animal ornament
To the Anasazi, who carved this ornament from jet, the frog symbolized adaptability.

Wheels, due to their similarity to the spoked wheels of the wagons that carried settlers into the heartlands of once-Native American territory. Each Medicine Wheel showed how different objects or qualities related to one another within the context of a greater whole, and how different forces and energies moved within it.

One Medicine Wheel might be regarded as the master wheel because it indicated balance within Nature and the most effective way of achieving harmony with the Universe and ourselves. It is upon this master Medicine Wheel (see pp.10–11) that Earth Medicine is structured.

Feast dish
Stylized bear carvings adorn this Tlingit feast dish. To the Native American, the bear symbolizes strength and self-sufficiency.

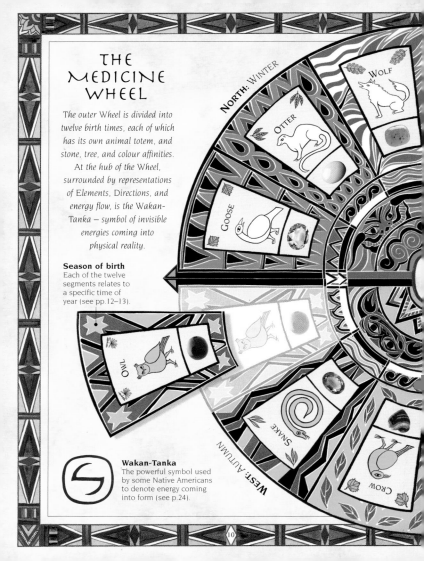

THE MEDICINE WHEEL

The outer Wheel is divided into twelve birth times, each of which has its own animal totem, and stone, tree, and colour affinities.

At the hub of the Wheel, surrounded by representations of Elements, Directions, and energy flow, is the Wakan-Tanka – symbol of invisible energies coming into physical reality.

Season of birth
Each of the twelve segments relates to a specific time of year (see pp.12–13).

Wakan-Tanka
The powerful symbol used by some Native Americans to denote energy coming into form (see p.24).

NORTH: WINTER

WEST: AUTUMN

WOLF

OTTER

GOOSE

OWL

SNAKE

CROW

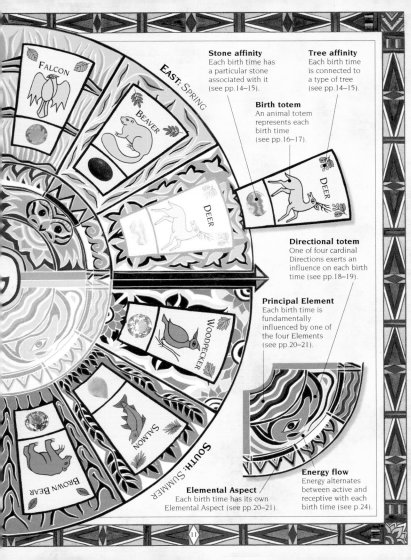

Stone affinity
Each birth time has a particular stone associated with it (see pp.14–15).

Tree affinity
Each birth time is connected to a type of tree (see pp.14–15).

Birth totem
An animal totem represents each birth time (see pp.16–17).

Directional totem
One of four cardinal Directions exerts an influence on each birth time (see pp.18–19).

Principal Element
Each birth time is fundamentally influenced by one of the four Elements (see pp.20–21).

Energy flow
Energy alternates between active and receptive with each birth time (see p.24).

Elemental Aspect
Each birth time has its own Elemental Aspect (see pp.20–21).

EAST: SPRING

SOUTH: SUMMER

FALCON

BEAVER

DEER

DEER

WOODPECKER

SALMON

BROWN BEAR

11

THE TWELVE
BIRTH TIMES

THE STRUCTURE OF THE MEDICINE WHEEL IS BASED UPON THE SEASONS TO REFLECT THE POWERFUL INFLUENCE OF NATURE ON HUMAN PERSONALITY.

The Medicine Wheel classifies human nature into twelve personality types, each corresponding to the characteristics of Nature at a particular time of the year. It is designed to act as a kind of map to help you discover your strengths and weaknesses, your inner drives and instinctive behaviours, and your true potential.

The four seasons form the basis of the Wheel's structure, with the Summer and Winter solstices and the Spring and Autumn equinoxes marking each season's passing. In Earth Medicine,

each season is a metaphor for a stage of human growth and development. Spring is likened to infancy and the newness of life; and Summer to the exuberance of youth and of rapid development. Autumn represents the fulfilment that mature adulthood brings, while Winter symbolizes the accumulated wisdom that can be drawn upon in later life.

Each seasonal quarter of the Wheel is further divided into three periods, making twelve time segments altogether. The time of your birth determines the direction from which

Seasonal rites

Performers at the Iroquois mid-Winter ceremony wore masks made of braided maize husks. They danced to attune themselves to energies that would ensure a good harvest.

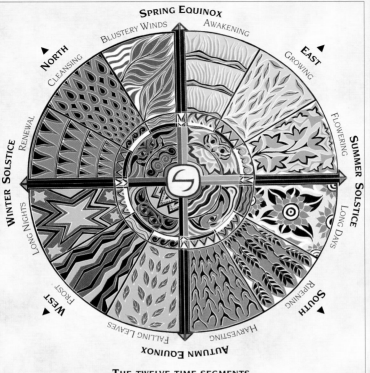

SPRING EQUINOX

BLUSTERY WINDS   AWAKENING

▲ NORTH   EAST ▲

Cleansing   GROWING

Renewal   FLOWERING

WINTER SOLSTICE   SUMMER SOLSTICE

LONG NIGHTS   LONG DAYS

WEST   SOUTH

FROST   RIPENING

FALLING LEAVES   HARVESTING

AUTUMN EQUINOX

THE TWELVE TIME SEGMENTS

you perceive life, and the qualities imbued in Nature in that season are reflected in your core character.

Each of the twelve time segments, or birth times, is named after a feature in the natural yearly cycle. For

example, the period after the Spring equinox is called Awakening time because it is the time of new growth, while the segment after the Autumn equinox is named after the falling leaves that characterize that time.

THE SIGNIFICANCE OF TOTEMS

NATIVE AMERICANS BELIEVED THAT TOTEMS – ANIMAL
SYMBOLS – REPRESENTED ESSENTIAL TRUTHS AND ACTED
AS CONNECTIONS TO NATURAL POWERS.

A totem is an animal or natural object adopted as an emblem to typify certain distinctive qualities. Native Americans regarded animals, whose behaviour is predictable, as particularly useful guides to categorizing human patterns of behaviour.

A totem mirrors aspects of your nature and unlocks the intuitive knowledge that lies beyond the reasoning capacity of the intellect. It may take the form of a carving or moulding, a pictorial image, or a token of fur, feather,

bone, tooth, or claw. Its presence serves as an immediate link with the energies it represents. A totem is therefore more effective than a glyph or symbol as an aid to comprehending non-physical powers and formative forces.

PRIMARY TOTEMS

In Earth Medicine you have three primary totems: a birth totem, a Directional totem, and an Elemental totem. Your *birth totem* is the embodiment of core characteristics that correspond with the dominant aspects of Nature during your birth time.

Symbol of strength
The handle of this Tlingit knife is carved with a raven and a bear head, symbols of insight and inner strength.

All twelve birth totems, each relating to a birth time, are described on pp.16–17.

Your *Directional totem* aligns you with your inner senses, which direct the main thrust of your endeavours. Each of the four seasons on the Wheel is compatible with one of the four Directions, and each of the Directions is represented by a totem. For example, Spring is associated with the East, where the sun rises, and signifies seeing things in new ways; its totem is the Eagle. The four

Prize totem

A chief or warrior of the Fox tribe affirmed his rank with this bear claw necklace.

Directional totems are explained on pp.18–19. Your *Elemental totem* relates to your instinctive behaviours. The qualities of the four Elements – Fire, Water, Earth, and Air – and their totems are introduced on pp.20–21.

THREE AFFINITIES

Each birth time also has an affinity with a tree, a stone, and a colour (see pp.36–41). These three affinities have qualities that can strengthen you during challenging times.

"If a man is to succeed, he must be governed not by his inclination, but by an understanding of the ways of animals..." Teton Sioux teaching

THE TWELVE
BIRTH TOTEMS

THE TWELVE BIRTH TIMES ARE REPRESENTED BY TOTEMS,
EACH ONE AN ANIMAL THAT BEST EXPRESSES THE
QUALITIES INHERENT IN THAT BIRTH TIME.

Earth Medicine associates an animal totem with each birth time (the two sets of dates below reflect the difference in season between the northern and southern hemispheres). These animals help to connect you to the powers and abilities that they represent. For an in-depth study of the Owl birth totem, see pp.28–29.

FALCON
21 March–19 April (N. Hem)
22 Sept–22 Oct (S. Hem)
Falcons are full of initiative, but often rush in to make decisions they may later regret. Lively and extroverted, they have enthusiasm for new experiences but can sometimes lack persistence.

DEER
21 May–20 June (N. Hem)
23 Nov–21 Dec (S. Hem)
Deer are willing to sacrifice the old for the new. They loathe routine, thriving on variety and challenges. They have a wild side, often leaping from one situation or relationship into another without reflection.

BEAVER
20 April–20 May (N. Hem)
23 Oct–22 Nov (S. Hem)
Practical and steady, Beavers have a capacity for perseverance. Good homemakers, they are warm and affectionate but need harmony and peace to avoid becoming irritable. They have a keen aesthetic sense.

WOODPECKER
21 June–21 July (N. Hem)
22 Dec–19 Jan (S. Hem)
Emotional and sensitive, Woodpeckers are warm to those closest to them, and willing to sacrifice their needs for those of their loved ones. They have lively imaginations but can be worriers.

SALMON

22 July–21 August (N. Hem)
20 Jan–18 Feb (S. Hem)

Enthusiastic and self-confident,
Salmon people enjoy running things.
They are uncompromising and
forceful, and can occasionally seem a
little arrogant or self-important. They
are easily hurt by neglect.

BROWN BEAR

22 August–21 Sept (N. Hem)
19 Feb–20 March (S. Hem)

Brown Bears are hardworking,
practical, and self-reliant. They do
not like change, preferring to stick
to what is familiar. They have a flair
for fixing things, are good-natured,
and make good friends.

CROW

22 Sept–22 Oct (N. Hem)
21 March–19 April (S. Hem)

Crows dislike solitude and feel most
comfortable in company. Although
usually pleasant and good-natured,
they can be strongly influenced by
negative atmospheres, becoming
gloomy and prickly.

SNAKE

23 Oct–22 Nov (N. Hem)
20 April–20 May (S. Hem)

Snakes are secretive and
mysterious, hiding their feelings
beneath a cool exterior. Adaptable,
determined, and imaginative, they
are capable of bouncing back from
tough situations encountered in life.

OWL

23 Nov–21 Dec (N. Hem)
21 May–20 June (S. Hem)

Owls need freedom of expression.
They are lively, self-reliant, and have
an eye for detail. Inquisitive and
adaptable, they have a tendency to
overextend themselves. Owls are
often physically courageous.

GOOSE

22 Dec–19 Jan (N. Hem)
21 June–21 July (S. Hem)

Goose people are far-sighted
idealists who are willing to explore
the unknown. They approach life with
enthusiasm, determined to fulfil their
dreams. They are perfectionists, and
can appear unduly serious.

OTTER

20 Jan–18 Feb (N. Hem)
22 July–21 August (S. Hem)

Otters are friendly, lively, and
perceptive. They feel inhibited by
too many rules and regulations,
which often makes them appear
eccentric. They like cleanliness and
order, and have original minds.

WOLF

19 Feb–20 March (N. Hem)
22 August–21 Sept (S. Hem)

Wolves are sensitive, artistic, and
intuitive – people to whom others
turn for help. They value freedom
and their own space, and are easily
affected by others. They are
philosophical, trusting, and genuine.

THE INFLUENCE OF THE
DIRECTIONS

ALSO KNOWN BY NATIVE AMERICANS AS THE FOUR
WINDS, THE INFLUENCE OF THE FOUR DIRECTIONS IS
EXPERIENCED THROUGH YOUR INNER SENSES.

Regarded as the "keepers" or "caretakers" of the Universe, the four Directions or alignments were also referred to by Native Americans as the four Winds because their presence was felt rather than seen.

DIRECTIONAL TOTEMS

In Earth Medicine, each Direction or Wind is associated with a season and a time of day. Thus the Autumn birth times – Falling Leaves time, Frost time, and Long Nights time –

all fall within the West Direction, and evening. The Direction to which your birth time belongs influences the nature of your inner senses.

The East Direction is associated with illumination. Its totem is the Eagle – a bird that soars closest to the Sun and can see clearly from height. The South is the Direction of Summer and the afternoon. It signifies growth and fruition, fluidity, and emotions. Its totem, the Mouse, symbolizes productivity, feelings, and an ability to perceive detail:

"Remember...the circle of the sky, the stars, the super-natural Winds breathing night and day...the four Directions." Pawnee teaching

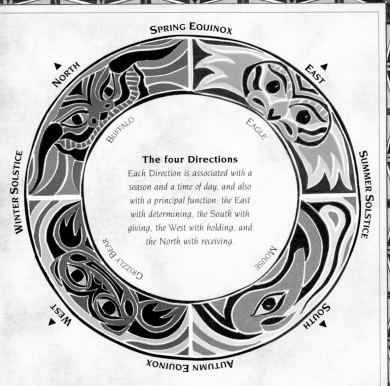

SPRING EQUINOX

NORTH

EAST

WINTER SOLSTICE

SUMMER SOLSTICE

BUFFALO

EAGLE

The four Directions
Each Direction is associated with a season and a time of day, and also with a principal function: the East with determining, the South with giving, the West with holding, and the North with receiving.

GRIZZLY BEAR

MOUSE

WEST

SOUTH

AUTUMN EQUINOX

The West is the Direction of Autumn and the evening. It signifies transformation – from day to night, from Summer to Winter – and the qualities of introspection and conservation. Its totem is the Grizzly Bear, which represents strength drawn from within. The North is the Direction of Winter and the night, and is associated with the mind and its sustenance – knowledge. Its totem is the Buffalo, an animal that was honoured by Native Americans as the great material "provider".

THE INFLUENCE OF THE
ELEMENTS

THE FOUR ELEMENTS — AIR, FIRE, WATER, AND EARTH —
PERVADE EVERYTHING AND INDICATE THE NATURE OF
MOVEMENT AND THE ESSENCE OF WHO YOU ARE.

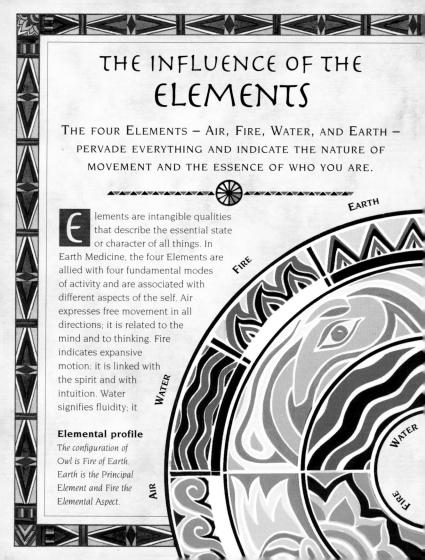

E lements are intangible qualities
that describe the essential state
or character of all things. In
Earth Medicine, the four Elements are
allied with four fundamental modes
of activity and are associated with
different aspects of the self. Air
expresses free movement in all
directions; it is related to the
mind and to thinking. Fire
indicates expansive
motion; it is linked with
the spirit and with
intuition. Water
signifies fluidity; it

Elemental profile
*The configuration of
Owl is Fire of Earth.
Earth is the Principal
Element and Fire the
Elemental Aspect.*

EARTH

FIRE

WATER

WATER

AIR

FIRE

has associations with the soul and the emotions. Earth symbolizes stability; it is related to the physical body and the sensations.

ELEMENTAL DISTRIBUTION

On the Medicine Wheel one Element is associated with each of the four Directions – Fire in the East, Earth in the West, Air in the North, and Water in the South. These are known as the Principal Elements.

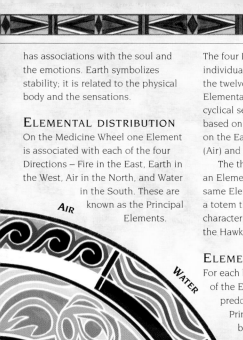

AIR

WATER

FIRE

EARTH

EARTH

AIR

The four Elements also have an individual association with each of the twelve birth times – known as the Elemental Aspects. They follow a cyclical sequence around the Wheel based on the action of the Sun (Fire) on the Earth, producing atmosphere (Air) and condensation (Water).

The three birth times that share an Elemental Aspect belong to the same Elemental family or "clan", with a totem that gives insight into its key characteristics. Owl people belong to the Hawk clan (see pp.34–35).

ELEMENTAL EMPHASIS

For each birth time, the qualities of the Elemental Aspect usually predominate over those of the Principal Element, although both are present to give a specific configuration, such as Fire of Earth (for Owl's, see pp.34–35). For Falcon, Woodpecker, and Otter, the Principal Element and the Elemental Aspect are identical (for example, Air of Air), so people of these totems tend to express that Element intensely.

THE INFLUENCE OF THE MOON

THE WAXING AND WANING OF THE MOON DURING ITS FOUR PHASES HAS A CRUCIAL INFLUENCE ON THE FORMATION OF PERSONALITY AND HUMAN ENDEAVOUR.

Native Americans regarded the Sun and Moon as indicators respectively of the active and receptive energies inherent in Nature (see p.24), as well as the measurers of time. They associated solar influences with conscious activity and the exercise of reason and the will, and lunar influences with subconscious activity and the emotional and intuitive aspects of human nature.

The Waxing Moon
This phase lasts for approximately eleven days. It is a time of growth and therefore ideal for developing new ideas and concentrating your efforts into new projects.

The Full Moon
Lasting about three days, this is when lunar power is at its height. It is therefore a good time for completing what was developed during the Waxing Moon.

THE FOUR PHASES

There are four phases in the twenty-nine-day lunar cycle, each one an expression of energy reflecting a particular mode of activity. They can be likened to the phases of growth of a flowering plant through the seasons: the emergence of buds (Waxing Moon), the bursting of flowers (Full Moon), the falling away of flowers (Waning Moon), and the germination of seeds (Dark Moon). The influence of each phase can be felt in two ways: in the formation of personality and in day-to-day life.

The energy expressed by the phase of the Moon at the time of your birth has a strong influence on personality. For instance, someone born during the Dark Moon is likely to be inward-looking, whilst a person born during the Full Moon may be more expressive. Someone born during a Waxing Moon is likely to have an outgoing nature, whilst a person born during a Waning Moon may be reserved. Consult a set of Moon tables to discover the phase the Moon was in on *your* birthday.

In your day-to-day life, the benefits of coming into harmony with the Moon's energies are considerable. Experience the energy of the four phases by consciously working with them. A Native American approach is described below.

The Waning Moon

A time for making changes, this phase lasts for an average of eleven days. Use it to improve and modify, and to dispose of what is no longer needed or wanted.

The Dark Moon

The Moon disappears from the sky for around four days. This is a time for contemplation of what has been achieved, and for germinating the seeds for the new.

THE INFLUENCE OF
ENERGY FLOW

THE MEDICINE WHEEL REFLECTS THE PERFECT
BALANCE OF THE COMPLEMENTARY ACTIVE AND
RECEPTIVE ENERGIES THAT CO-EXIST IN NATURE.

E nergy flows through
Nature in two comple-
mentary ways, which can
be expressed in terms of active
and receptive, or male and female.
The active energy principle is
linked with the Elements of Fire
and Air, and the receptive
principle with Water and Earth.

Each of the twelve birth times
has an active or receptive energy
related to its Elemental Aspect.
Travelling around the Wheel, the
two energies alternate with each
birth time, resulting in an equal
balance of active and receptive
energies, as in Nature.

Active energy is associated
with the Sun and conscious
activity. Those whose birth times
take this principle prefer to pursue
experience. They are conceptual,

energetic, outgoing, practical, and
analytical. Receptive energy is
associated with the Moon and
subconscious activity. Those
whose birth times take this
principle prefer to attract
experience. They are intuitive,
reflective, conserving, emotional,
and nurturing.

THE WAKAN-TANKA

At the heart of the Wheel lies
an S-shape within a circle, the
symbol of the life-giving source
of everything that comes into
physical existence – seemingly out
of nothing. Named by the Plains
Indians as Wakan-Tanka (Great
Power), it can also be perceived
as energy coming into form and
form reverting to energy in the
unending continuity of life.

OWL
MEDICINE
YOUR IN-DEPTH
PERSONALITY PROFILE

SEASON OF BIRTH
LONG NIGHTS TIME

THE PENETRATING WINDS OF AUTUMN CAN BE FELT IN
THE THIRD BIRTH TIME OF THE SEASON, LENDING THOSE
BORN THEN CLARITY OF MIND AND LOVE OF FREEDOM.

Long Nights time is one of the twelve birth times, the fundamental division of the year into twelve seasonal segments (see pp.12–13). As the third period of the Autumn cycle it is the time of the year when the nights are longest and the power of the Sun is at its weakest. The air is crisp, and the winds chilling, often heralding the arrival of the first flurries of snow.

INFLUENCE OF NATURE
The qualities and characteristics imbued in Nature at this time form the basis of your own nature. So, just as the cool air makes the atmosphere clear and clean, so, if you were born during Long Nights time, you possess a keen eye for detail together with a clarity of thought that enables you to perceive all the options open to you, even in times of confusion, and to set your sights on long-term goals. Like the cool winds of the season, you enjoy freedom of movement and freedom of expression, and resent any attempts to confine or limit you.

This is the season in which the hours of darkness are far greater than those of daylight, and you are drawn to that which is hidden or secret. Your intuitive powers are extremely strong and you often realize the truth of a situation before it becomes obvious to others. Your affinity for the darkness is also reflected in your tendency to withdraw from people or situations when you feel your freedom is threatened.

STAGE OF LIFE

This time of year might be compared to the maturity of late middle age. In human development terms, it is a period in which the wisdom derived from life's experiences finds embodiment in the achievement of true individuality of spirit and expression, and the understanding of complex or otherwise mysterious matters.

ACHIEVE YOUR POTENTIAL

Your lively and enquiring mind together with your confident, independent spirit, gives you a vigorous nature that requires freedom to explore. Alert and inquisitive, you tend to develop many varied interests and pioneer fresh ways of working. Confident of your ideas, you

Nature's energy

Nature brings to a close its reflective phase in this, the last cycle of Autumn before the Winter solstice. Chill, penetrating winds clear the air, and the number of daylight hours fall to the lowest of the year.

enjoy discussing them at length with others. Most of the time others find your characteristic boldness of expression refreshing and sincere, but try to remember that being overly frank may be hurtful to those less confident than yourself.

You prize freedom to be yourself above all else, but try to ensure that this does not result in selfish and insensitive behaviour, or in running away from difficult situations or burdensome responsibilities.

"Life is a circle from childhood to childhood; so it is with everything where power moves." **Black Elk teaching**

BIRTH TOTEM
THE OWL

THE ESSENTIAL NATURE AND CHARACTERISTIC BEHAVIOUR OF THE OWL EXPRESSES THE PERSONALITY TYPE OF THOSE BORN DURING LONG NIGHTS TIME.

Like the owl, people born during Long Nights time are inquisitive, intuitive, and observant. If you were born at this time, you have an enquiring mind and outgoing nature, which thrives on freedom and adventure.

Independent and perceptive, you require freedom of movement and expression to satisfy your lively, cheerful disposition and inquisitive mind. Your dislike of limitations or love of the grand gesture occasionally leads you to evade your responsibilities or voice your opinions insensitively.

Clear-thinking with a keen eye for detail and an investigative approach to life, you have the ability to discover new ways of perceiving situations, and to present innovative methods of working. Others are quick to follow your confident and enthusiastic lead. You value honesty and integrity highly, and enjoy uncovering information previously shrouded in secrecy and bringing it out into the open for all to see.

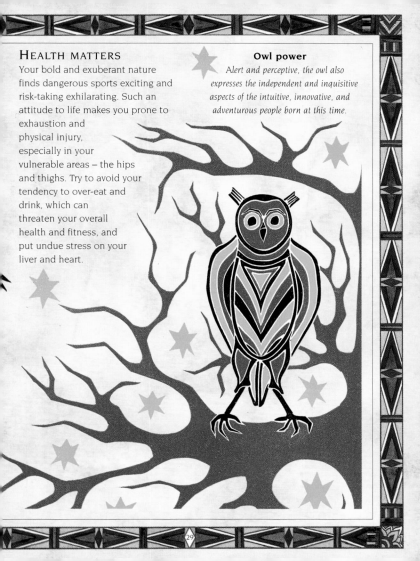

HEALTH MATTERS

Your bold and exuberant nature finds dangerous sports exciting and risk-taking exhilarating. Such an attitude to life makes you prone to exhaustion and physical injury, especially in your vulnerable areas – the hips and thighs. Try to avoid your tendency to over-eat and drink, which can threaten your overall health and fitness, and put undue stress on your liver and heart.

Owl power

Alert and perceptive, the owl also expresses the independent and inquisitive aspects of the intuitive, innovative, and adventurous people born at this time.

THE OWL AND
RELATIONSHIPS

LIVELY AND FLAMBOYANT, OWL PEOPLE ARE OFTEN
VERY POPULAR. THEY MAKE WARM AND EXCITING
PARTNERS BUT MAY BE RELUCTANT TO SETTLE DOWN.

houghtful, reflective Owl people, like their totem animal, enjoy a reputation for wisdom. If your birth totem is Owl, your powers of perception make you valued for your insight, while your pioneering nature means you often attract followers, both socially and at work. However, your boldness can make you seem irresponsible, making others act with caution around you. You can also be tactless – try to temper your frankness with compassion and sensitivity.

LOVING RELATIONSHIPS
Although Owl people need close relationships, they resent feeling tied down and may take a long time to commit to a partner. Male Owl craves excitement, while female Owl is a devoted partner once she has

met her match. Both are flirtatious romantics, and need an adventurous sex life if they are not to grow bored.

When problems occur, this often arises from your tendency to rebel if you feel restricted. Your dislike of commitment can make your partner feel insecure. Try making the effort to show that your need for freedom does not signal a lack of love.

COPING WITH OWL
Owl people are not easily swayed, so be sure of your facts if you want to win them round to your point of view. They need time alone as much as they need air, so do not take their sudden withdrawal as a personal rejection. The best way to handle Owl people is to give them space and the freedom to express themselves – hold too tight and you'll lose them.

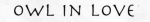

OWL IN LOVE

Owl with Falcon This can be a warm and fulfilling partnership provided there is a mutual respect for each other's individuality.

Owl with Beaver Beaver can make Owl's life more fun, but if Beaver becomes too smothering, Owl might feel inclined to flee the nest.

Owl with Deer Deer's sexuality can keep Owl held in a long-lasting relationship. Both can be adaptable to each other's needs.

Owl with Woodpecker Owl may respond to the warmth of Woodpecker's nurturing but will feel caged if it turns into possessiveness.

Owl with Salmon These two may share a determination and passion that will satisfy each other's needs and lead them into new experiences.

Owl with Brown Bear A stable match that does not depend on sexual intimacy, but it can be full of surprises.

Owl with Crow If they can commit without feeling too confined, they can bring out the best in each other.

Owl with Snake In spite of their initial attraction, long-term commitment will need patience and compromise.

Owl with Owl A relationship that is unlikely to grow boring for it holds promise of stimulating activity. It's the routine side of life that will present the difficulties.

Owl with Goose Goose may yearn for love, but Owl might be reluctant to make a commitment, especially to one who can be restrictive.

Owl with Otter A spirited but comfortable relationship in which each is able to share the other's fantasies.

Owl with Wolf Wolf's self-sacrificing nature may seem at odds with Owl's desire to do what he or she wants, but both can be romantic and so keep life sparkling.

DIRECTIONAL TOTEM
THE GRIZZLY BEAR

THE GRIZZLY BEAR SYMBOLIZES THE INFLUENCE OF THE WEST ON OWL PEOPLE, WHO HAVE THE CLARITY OF MIND AND INNER STRENGTH TO ACHIEVE THEIR GOALS.

Falling Leaves time, Frost time, and Long Nights time all fall within the quarter of the Medicine Wheel associated with the West Direction or Wind.

The West is aligned with Autumn and dusk, and it is associated with introspection, consolidation, maturity, and the wisdom that stems from experience. The power of the West's influence is primarily with the physical, and its principal function is the power of holding. It takes as its totem the self-sufficient grizzly bear.

The specific influence of the West on Owl people is on clarity of purpose, enabling you to cope with change and to find an outlet for your

Grizzly bear bowl
This Tlingit wooden bowl is carved in the shape of a bear, which is associated with inner strength.

creative powers. It is a penetrating Wind, releasing your potential and sharpening your innate ability to impart wisdom to others.

GRIZZLY CHARACTERISTICS

In Autumn, the powerful grizzly bear makes careful preparation for hibernation, storing up its inner strength for reawakening in Spring. Hence, Native Americans associated it with resourcefulness and self-reliance. It was seen as introspective because it seemed to be thoughtful about its actions; as a totem, it encourages you to look within for guidance and to learn from the past to bring wisdom to your decisions.

If your Directional totem is Grizzly Bear, you are likely to have a capacity for endurance, the resolve to face up to your weaknesses, and the courage to learn from experience.

The spirit of the West
The Sun sets in the West, symbolizing reflection; the Grizzly Bear totem signifies self-reliance.

ELEMENTAL TOTEM
THE HAWK

LIKE THE HAWK, WHICH SOARS THROUGH THE SKY AT SPEED, OWL PEOPLE'S ADVENTUROUS AND SELF-RELIANT SPIRIT REQUIRES FREEDOM OF EXPRESSION.

The Elemental Aspect of Owl people is Fire. They share this Aspect with Falcon and Salmon people, who all therefore belong to the same Elemental family or "clan" (see pp.20–21 for an introduction to the influence of the Elements). Each Elemental clan has a totem to provide insight into its essential characteristics.

THE HAWK CLAN

The totem of the Elemental clan of Fire is Hawk, which symbolizes an impulsive and enthusiastic nature with a pioneering spirit.

The hawk is quick and clear-sighted, swooping on its prey suddenly, seizing every opportunity. So, if you belong to this clan, you have a lively personality and are happy to take the lead. You also have

Spark of vitality
The hawk symbolizes the key qualities of Fire: energy and enthusiasm.

an eye for detail and intuitive powers of understanding.

Individualistic, courageous, and creative, you are excited by fresh ventures, and fire others with your enthusiasm. You dislike feeling restricted, bored, or stuck in routine. You are often motivated by sudden flashes of inspiration, so you crave stimulation and new challenges to capture your imagination.

ELEMENTAL PROFILE

For Owl people, the predominant Elemental Aspect of enthusiastic Fire is fundamentally affected by the qualities of your Principal Element – persistent Earth. So, if you were born at this time, you are likely to have a bold, idealistic, and outgoing personality, coupled with the stability needed to translate your ideas and ideals into tangible results.

Despite this, you may have a tendency to over-extend yourself and dissipate your energies, driven by

Fire of Earth
The Element of Fire feeds Earth, generating enthusiasm tempered by stability.

the ardour of Fire and the persistence of Earth. So you may sometimes find yourself feeling exhausted or frustrated because you have achieved less than you originally envisaged. At times like these, or when you are feeling low, try the following revitalizing exercise. Your affinity with Fire means you respond well to the warming energy of the Sun, or to the air that has been cleansed by a storm. Find a quiet, open spot outside, away from traffic pollution and other people. In Winter, sit by an open fire and look into the heart of the flames.

Breathe slowly and deeply, letting the brightness of the Sun or the fire warm you. With each in-breath, feel the energizing power of the life-force bringing you inner light, recharging your body, mind, and spirit, refreshing your whole being.

STONE AFFINITY
OBSIDIAN

By using the gemstone with which your own essence resonates, you can tap into the power of the Earth itself and awaken your inner strengths.

Gemstones are minerals that are formed within the Earth itself in an exceedingly slow but continuous process. Native Americans valued gemstones not only for their beauty but also for being literally part of the Earth, and therefore possessing part of its life-force. They regarded gemstones as being "alive" – channellers of energy that could be used in many ways: to heal, to protect, or for meditation.

Every gemstone has a different energy or vibration. On the Medicine Wheel, a stone is associated with each birth time, the energy of which

Polished obsidian
The vibrations of obsidian are believed to soothe the emotions and help stabilize both internal and external energies.

resonates with the essence of those born during that time. Because of this energy affiliation, your stone can help bring you into harmony with the Earth and create balance within yourself. It can enhance and develop your good qualities and endow you with the qualities or abilities you need.

ENERGY RESONANCE

Owl people have an affinity with obsidian – a natural glass formed from volcanic lava; it is usually black and may be striped or spotted. Its origins deep within the Earth make it a good grounding stone, providing stability and protection from harm.

ACTIVATE YOUR GEMSTONE

Obtain a piece of obsidian and cleanse it by holding it under cold running water. Allow it to dry naturally, then, holding the stone with both hands, bring it up to your mouth and blow into it sharply and hard three or four times in order to impregnate it with your breath. Next, hold it firmly in one hand and silently welcome it into your life as a friend and helper.

When you are unclear about which direction you should take to find fulfilment, use the obsidian to help you meditate. Find a quiet spot to sit without fear of interruption and place the obsidian in front of you at a level where you can gaze at it without strain. Focus on the stone, and let yourself receive any guidance about the direction you should take. Listen for the quiet voice of your inner self.

Obsidian is sometimes known as "Apache tears" – the Apache women wept copiously after their men were massacred and legend says that their tears became embedded in black stone. Obsidian is said to bring comfort from sadness and grief.

If your birth totem is Owl, you will find obsidian sharpens your inner vision, enabling you to cut straight to the heart of the matter when faced with a difficult problem.

Obsidian power
To help protect yourself from harmful influences, wear or carry a piece of obsidian at all times.

"The outline of the stone is round; the power of the stone is endless." Lakota Sioux teaching

TREE AFFINITY
HONEYSUCKLE

GAIN A DEEPER UNDERSTANDING OF YOUR OWN NATURE
AND AWAKEN POWERS LYING DORMANT WITHIN YOU BY
RESPECTING AND CONNECTING WITH YOUR AFFINITY TREE.

Trees have an important part to play in the protection of Nature's mechanisms and in the maintenance of the Earth's atmospheric balance, which is essential for the survival of the human race.

Native Americans referred to trees as "Standing People" because they stand firm, obtaining strength from their connection with the Earth. They therefore teach us the importance of being grounded, whilst at the same time listening to, and reaching for, our higher aspirations. When respected as living beings, trees can provide insight into the workings of Nature and our own inner selves.

On the Medicine Wheel, each birth time is associated with a particular kind of tree, the basic qualities of which complement the nature of those born during that time. Owl people have an affinity with the honeysuckle. This twining, vigorous climber forms a mass of labyrinthine twigs – symbolic of the quest for hidden secrets, which are also alluring to the Owl. The heady

CONNECT WITH YOUR TREE

Appreciate the beauty of your affinity tree and study its nature carefully, for it has an affinity with your own nature.

The vigorous honeysuckle climbs by twining itself around a support, covering it with its dense growth. Its tubular flowers, sometimes white or creamy-yellow, sometimes flushed purple or red, are justly renowned for their delicious scent.

Try the following exercise when you need to revitalize your inner strength. Stand beside your affinity tree. Place the palms of your hands on the plant or gently but firmly hold a leaf in each hand. Inhale slowly and experience energy from the tree's roots flow through your body. If easily available, obtain a cutting or twig from your affinity tree to keep as a totem or helper.

fragrance of its flowers and sinuous habit of its growth make it a sensual plant, loved by hedonistic Owls. When Owl people feel they are losing sight of their goals, they can tap into their own energy and inner strength by connecting with the honeysuckle (see panel above).

CLEAR COMMITMENT

If your birth totem is Owl, you are confident and adventurous, but you often dissipate your energy by

chasing too many leads at once. Your wide-ranging interests and dislike of commitment can mean you lack the deep fulfilment you truly crave.

Just as the unruly honeysuckle gives of its best when trained and tied in, so you can find within you the power to be focused and single-minded as you pursue your goals. Call on the honeysuckle's help and draw on its energy to help you renew your clarity of mind and purpose and channel your adventurous spirit.

"All healing plants are given by Wakan-Tanka; therefore they are holy." Lakota Sioux teaching

COLOUR AFFINITY
GOLD

Enhance your positive qualities by using the power of your affinity colour to affect your emotional and mental states.

Each birth time has an affinity with a particular colour. This is the colour that resonates best with the energies of the people born during that time. Exposure to your affinity colour will encourage a positive emotional and mental response, while exposure to colours that clash with your affinity colour will have a negative effect on your sense of well-being.

Gold resonates with Owl people. A symbol of affluence and durability, gold suggests the possession of earthly riches, and the independence, power, and freedom that accompanies material wealth. It is the embodiment of comfort and well-being and stimulates the dynamic pursuit of excellence and the ambition to fulfil your dreams and aspirations. It

Colour scheme
Experience the full benefit of your colour affinity. Let a gold colour theme be the thread that runs through your home, from the cushions and table settings to the walls and floors.

REFLECT ON YOUR COLOUR

Take three gold-coloured candles. Stand in the centre of a room and position the candles around you to form the corners of a triangle which is a natural amplifier.

Light each candle in turn to release its colour energy into the atmosphere. Sit down and relax, ensuring that you are facing one of the points of the triangle. Enjoy the atmosphere of tranquillity in the room and focus all your attention on the colour. Breathe slowly and rhythmically and feel the golden light filtering through your entire body, energizing every cell. Allow any thoughts and sensations to flow through your mind and body, and reflect on them.

arouses warmth and compassion towards others, determination to succeed, freedom of spirit and expression, and abundant quantities of self-confidence.

Colour benefits

Strengthen your aura and enhance your positive qualities by introducing tints of gold to the interior decor of your home. Spots of colour can make all the difference. For example, a gold motif on the curtains or wallpaper can alter the ambience of a room, or try placing vibrant orange flowers or gold-sprayed cones in a golden vase or dish.

If you need a confidence boost, wear something that contains gold. Whenever your energies are low, practise the colour reflection exercise outlined above, to balance your emotions, awaken your creativity, and help you to feel joyful.

"The power of the spirit should be honoured with its colour." *Lakota Sioux teaching*

WORKING THE WHEEL
LIFE PATH

CONSIDER YOUR BIRTH PROFILE AS A STARTING POINT IN THE DEVELOPMENT OF YOUR CHARACTER AND THE ACHIEVEMENT OF PERSONAL FULFILMENT.

Each of the twelve birth times is associated with a particular path of learning, or with a collection of lessons to be learned through life. By following your path of learning you will develop strengths in place of weaknesses, achieve a greater sense of harmony with the world, and discover inner peace.

YOUR PATH OF LEARNING
For Owl people, the first lesson on your path of learning is to cultivate a more responsible attitude to life. Try to overcome your fear of commitment and your tendency to run away from ties and responsibilities. Recognize that it is you and not fate that decides the way you live, the sort of work you do, and the quality of your relationships. Problems rarely disappear simply because you ignore them, so next time you have a difficult decision to make, face up to

"Each man's road is shown to him within his own heart. There he sees all the truths of life." Cheyenne teaching

the responsibility. By steering your own course through life, you will gain in confidence and win the respect of others.

Owl people also need to learn how to concentrate their energies on the achievement of a few well-chosen goals. Exuberant and energetic, you tend to dissipate your energies by pursuing too many separate paths at once. As a consequence, many of your ideas or dreams do not achieve their full potential. Try to focus your energies on the pursuit of a select number of clear-cut goals.

Your third lesson is to learn to be more sensitive to the feelings of others. Bold and courageous, you sometimes hurt others by your tactless comments or lack of understanding of their needs. Try to show more compassion towards those more fearful and less strong than you. Not everyone thrives on excitement and adventure.

WORKING THE WHEEL
MEDICINE POWER

HARNESS THE POWERS OF OTHER BIRTH TIMES TO
TRANSFORM YOUR WEAKNESSES INTO STRENGTHS AND
MEET THE CHALLENGES IN YOUR LIFE.

Complementary affinity
*A key strength of Deer – weak in
Owl – is the ability to adapt
ideals to everyday life.*

The whole spectrum of human qualities and abilities is represented on the Medicine Wheel. The totems and affinities associated with each birth time indicate the basic qualities with which those born at that time are equipped.

Study your path of learning (see pp.42–43) to identify those aspects of your personality that may need to be strengthened, then look at other birth times to discover the totems and affinities that can assist you in this task. For example, your Elemental profile is Fire of Earth (see pp.34–35), so for balance you need the freedom and clarity of Air

and the adaptive nature of Water. Otter's Elemental profile is Air of Air and Wolf's is Water of Air, so meditate on these birth totems. In addition, you may find it useful to study the profiles of the other two members of your Elemental clan of Hawk – Falcon and Salmon – to discover how the same Elemental Aspect can be expressed differently.

Also helpful is the birth totem that sits opposite yours on the Medicine Wheel, which contains qualities that complement or enhance your own. This is known as your complementary affinity, which for Owl people is Deer.

ESSENTIAL STRENGTHS

Described below are the essential strengths of each birth totem. To develop a quality that is weak in yourself or that you need to meet a particular challenge, meditate upon the birth totem that contains the attribute you need. Obtain a representation of the relevant totem – a claw, tooth, or feather; a picture, ring, or model. Affirm that the power it represents is within you.

Falcon medicine is the power of keen observation and the ability to act decisively and energetically whenever action is required.

Beaver medicine is the ability to think creatively and laterally – to develop alternative ways of doing or thinking about things.

Deer medicine is characterized by sensitivity to the intentions of others and to that which might be detrimental to your well-being.

Woodpecker medicine is the ability to establish a steady rhythm throughout life and to be tenacious in protecting all that you hold dear.

Salmon medicine is the strength to be determined and courageous in the choice of goals you want to achieve and to have enough stamina to see a task through to the end.

Brown Bear medicine is the ability to be resourceful, hardworking, and dependable in times of need, and to draw on inner strength.

Crow medicine is the ability to transform negative or non-productive situations into positive ones and to transcend limitations.

Snake medicine is the talent to adapt easily to changes in circumstances and to manage transitional phases well.

Owl medicine is the power to see clearly during times of uncertainty and to conduct life consistently, according to long-term plans.

Goose medicine is the courage to do whatever might be necessary to protect your ideals and adhere to your principles in life.

Otter medicine is the ability to connect with your inner child, to be innovative and idealistic, and to thoroughly enjoy the ordinary tasks and routines of everyday life.

Wolf medicine is the courage to act according to your intuition and instincts rather than your intellect, and to be compassionate.